MINE  libs

Welcome to Mine-Libs, a Minecraft-themed ad-lib book!

This book follows the traditional ad-lib game rules. The first page of each story will have a list of words for you to fill in. Don't turn the page yet! Fill in each word, either by yourself or with friends. Then, when you've written down the silliest words you can think of, turn the page and put each word in the story, with hilarious results!

If you enjoy these stories, we suggest you check out "Steve and Bleater Build a House," for more adventures between these two best friends.

THE UNOFFICIAL MINECRAFT LEGACY SERIES
Vol. 1
Steve & Bleater Build a House

Tips on how to fill out this book

Noun: A noun is a word that is a person, place, or thing.
It's usually something you can touch like Spiderman,
a house, or a water bottle.

Plural Noun: The same as above but more than one, like houses
or water bottles.

Adjective: Adjectives describe nouns.
What does your house look like? Is it big, blue, silly,
beautiful or terrible? What about your water bottle?
Is it teeny-tiny, golden, loud or funny?

Verb: Verbs describe actions.
Some examples are jump, run, flip, bake, build, and mine.

Verb ending in "-ing": Same as above but add "-ing" at the end.
Jumping, running, flipping, baking, building and mining.

Adverb: Adverbs describe verbs, and usually end with "-ly."
For example: quickly, slowly, noisily, grumpily, lazily.

Exclamation: These are words that you say when you are
surprised, or scared, or when you want to impress
your enemies like "Ka-pow!" or "Bang!" or "Yowza!"
or even "Cowabunga!"

Some of the other words are more obvious like:
Body Parts (ears, feet, nose),
Shape (circle, diamond, square),
Place (the ocean, Times Square, the Bermuda Triangle),
Animals and animal noises (horse, cow, baaaa, moooo).

Remember, the sillier the word, the funnier the story!

Hi, my name is Steve!

Plural noun _____

Boy's name _____

Someone in the room _____

Shape _____

Body part _____

Shape _____

Shape _____

Adverb _____

Adjective _____

Exclamation! _____

Noun _____

Noun _____

Mood _____

Hi, my name is Steve!

Hello _____, my name is _____.
        Plural noun   *Boy's name*

You may have noticed that I'm not shaped like

_____. I have a/an _____ head,
Someone in the room   *Shape*

square _____, _____ arms and
              Body part   *Shape*

legs...well...actually, I'm all _____. I don't
                                      Shape

mind that my arms and legs move _____.
                                        Adverb

Even though I am square, I'm actually a pretty

_____ swimmer. Though if I stay still, I start
      Adjective

to sink. Sometimes people say: "_____! Is
                                      Exclamation!

that a smile on your face, or a/an _____?"
                                          Noun

It's a/an _____ of course, because I'm al-
              Noun

ways so _____!
              Mood

My Best Friend

Noun _____

Animal _____

Plural noun _____

Noun _____

Verb _____

Adjective _____

Adjective _____

Verb ending in "-ing" _____

Adjective _____

Plural noun _____

Verb ending in "-ed" _____

Adjective ending in -"est" _____

Noun _____

Plural noun _____

Adjective _____

My Best Friend

My best _____ in the whole world is
         Noun

a/an _____ named Bleater. We've been
      Animal

together since we were tiny _____. No
                                Plural noun

matter what happens in _____, I know I can
                           Noun

count on Bleater to _____ by my side. Even
                       Verb

in the face of danger, he is always _____
                                       Adjective

and _____. We once fought a skeleton to-
      Adjective

gether. By fought, I mean ran away _____,
                                      Verb ending in "-ing"

of course. Without him, my life would be very

_____. Together, we have explored the
  Adjective

tallest _____. We have _____
         Plural noun   Verb ending in "-ed"

into the _____ caverns. We have mined
          Adjective ending in "-est"

everything from plain old _____ to beau-
                             Noun

tiful, sparkly _____. The only thing that
                 Plural noun

Bleater hates is getting wet. I hate it, too, because it

makes him smell _____.
                   Adjective

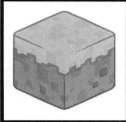

Welcome to the World!

Adjective _____

Plural noun _____

Plural noun _____

Place (plural) _____

Place (plural) _____

Noun _____

Noun _____

Place _____

Verb _____

Direction _____

Plural noun _____

Adjective _____

Adjective _____

Welcome to the World!

Welcome to the _____ world of Mine-
Adjective

craft! There are a few _____ you need to
Plural noun

know. The world is separated into different areas

called _____. There are _____,
Plural noun   Place (plural)

deserts, _____, mountains, and many
Place (plural)

more. There is also a whole _____ under the
Noun

ground. In Minecraft, you can mine almost anything

you can see, from the _____, to the trees,
Noun

to the _____. Better than that, you can
Place

craft anything you want! If you can _____
Verb

it, you can probably craft it! Oh, one last thing you

need to know--when the sun goes _____,
Direction

that's when the _____ come out. You'll
Plural noun

want to find somewhere _____ to hide
Adjective

out, until you're _____ enough to fight.
Adjective

Tools

Number _____

Plural noun _____

Verb ending in "-ing" _____

Noun _____

Verb ending in "-ing" _____

Adverb ending in "-er" _____

Noun _____

Verb ending in "-ing" _____

Noun _____

Noun _____

Noun _____

Adjective _____

Plural noun _____

Noun _____

Verb ending in "-ing" _____

Plural noun _____

Plural noun _____

Tools

Tools are essential for any kind mining. There are

_____ basic type(s) of tools: axes, _____,
  Number   *Plural noun*

pickaxes, and hoes. Axes are used for _____
                                              Verb ending in "-ing"

wood. Sure, you can punch a/an _____ with
                                         Noun

your fist, but _____ an axe will make the work
                  Verb ending in "-ing"

much _____ and easier. The same goes for dig-
        Adverb ending in "-er"

ging. Using a/an _____ will increase your speed
                    Noun

when _____ sand, gravel, or _____.
        Verb ending in "-ing"   *Noun*

Pickaxes are the perfect _____ for anything
                              Noun

harder than _____. Stone and ores are super
                Noun

_____ without a pickaxe, and some ores can only
  Adjective

be mined with pickaxes made from certain _____.
                                                Plural noun

For instance, only diamond pickaxes can be used to mine

_____. Hoes are only used for _____,
  Noun   *Verb ending in "-ing"*

they can make _____ in dirt which enable you to
                  Plural noun

plant _____.
        Plural noun

Trees and Wood

Plural noun _____

Noun _____

Plural noun _____

Plural noun _____

Hot place _____

Noun _____

Adjective ending in "-est" _____

Adjective ending in "-est" _____

Adjective _____

Noun _____

Adjective _____

Plural noun _____

Plural noun _____

Noun _____

Trees and Wood

Chances are you spawned somewhere with lots of _____. Trees provide a basic resource
Plural noun

that you need: _____! Wood is used to
Noun

make planks for building _____, sticks for
Plural noun

crafting tools and _____, and can even be
Plural noun

made into charcoal in a/an _____. There
Hot place

are many different types of wood, and they only

real difference is the _____. Birch is the
Noun

_____, and Dark Oak is the _____.
Adjective ending in "-est"   *Adjective ending in "-est"*

If you chop down a/an _____ tree (don't
Adjective

forget to use a/an _____!), you might also
Noun

get _____ and find some _____.
Adjective   *Plural noun*

You can plant these saplings to grow even more

_____—Minecraft trees are a totally
Plural noun

renewable _____!
Noun

Mining

Noun _____

Verb _____

Noun _____

Noun _____

Noun _____

Adjective ending in "-er" _____

Place (plural) _____

Adjective _____

Place _____

Place (plural) _____

Verb _____

Adjective _____

Noun _____

Plural noun _____

Same as above _____

Mining

Mining is a fact of life in Minecraft. It's the basic

_____ to get the items you need.
Noun

What you mine is what you _____. If you
Verb

mine a tree, you get _____. If you mine dirt,
Noun

you get _____. If you mine _____,
Noun   Noun

you get stone. The better your tools, the faster and

_____ mining will be. You can mine high on
Adjective ending in "-er"

_____, in the _____ grasslands, or
Place (plural)   Adjective

deep under the _____ in dark _____.
Place   Place (plural)

You can even _____ underwater! Here's
Verb

a general rule: the more dangerous the mining, the

_____ the items you're likely to find. So the
Adjective

best items—like diamonds and _____ —are
Noun

found way down underground. But down there, you

have to be careful of mobs and _____ —burn-
Plural noun

ing, hot, molten _____. Happy mining!
Same as above

Ores

Noun _____

Adjective ending in "-est" _____

Verb ending in "-ing" _____

Noun _____

Adjective _____

Plural noun _____

Plural noun _____

Adjective _____

Plural noun _____

Verb _____

Adjective ending in "-est" _____

Adjective ending in "-er" _____

Verb ending in "-ed" _____

Ores

Let me tell you all about ores. Ores are special types of _____ that you can find while mining.
Noun

The _____ kind of ore to find is coal. It's
Adjective ending in "-est"
everywhere! Coal is important for _____
Verb ending in "-ing"
torches, which provide _____. The second most
Noun
common ore is iron. Iron is used to make _____
Adjective
weapons and _____, as well as minecarts,
Plural noun
buckets, and _____. If you're lucky you
Plural noun
might find some gold ore. Gold is useful for many

_____ gadgets, like clocks and _____.
Adjective   *Plural noun*
If you're very lucky, you might _____ some
Verb
diamond ore! Diamonds are the best material in all of
Minecraft. Diamonds make the _____ armor!
Adjective ending in "-est"
The only thing _____ than diamonds are
Adjective ending in "-er"
emeralds. Emeralds can be _____ in villages
Verb ending in "-ed"
for even more useful items.

First Steps (Part I)

Adjective _____

Number _____

Verb ending in "-ing" _____

Number _____

Plural noun _____

Adjective _____

Plural noun _____

Verb _____

Adjective _____

Noun _____

Plural noun _____

Verb _____

Noun _____

First Steps (Part I)

Okay, so you've spawned into a _____
_{Adjective}
world. You only have _____ hour(s) un-
_{Number}
til the sun sets and mobs are _____
_{Verb ending in "-ing"}
all over the place. So what do you do? Priority
number _____ is to get some decent
_{Number}
_____. See that _____ tree over
_{Plural noun}   _{Adjective}
there? Punch it! Once you've mined a few wood
_____, you'll be able to _____
_{Plural noun}   _{Verb}
a crafting table and some _____ tools,
_{Adjective}
especially an axe and a/an _____. With
_{Noun}
the pickaxe, you'll be able to quickly upgrade your
_____ to stone. Mine enough wood to
_{Plural noun}
_____ a basic shelter, and you'll be sure
_{Verb}
to survive your first _____!
_{Noun}

First Steps (Part II)

Plural noun _____

Adjective _____

Verb ending in "-ing" _____

Adjective _____

Adjective _____

Noun _____

Number _____

Verb ending in "-ing" _____

Noun _____

Adjective _____

Adjective _____

Animal (plural) _____

Adjective _____

Noun _____

First Steps (Part II)

Now that you have a shelter and some

_____, it's time to find coal. Coal is use-
_{Plural noun}

ful for making torches and keeping your furnace

_____. Start by _____ nearby
_{Adjective} _{Verb ending in "-ing"}

for _____ rock faces or _____
_{Adjective} _{Adjective}

caves. If you're lucky, you might even find some

_____ without having to mine any
_{Noun}

other blocks. Once you've gathered _____
_{Number}

stack(s) of coal, spend the rest of the day

_____ for _____. You'll first
_{Verb ending in "-ing"} _{Noun}

need to craft a/an _____ sword, unless
_{Adjective}

you were extra _____ and found some
_{Adjective}

iron. Look for chickens, pigs, and _____.
_{Animal (plural)}

They're _____ to find, and will provide
_{Adjective}

plenty of _____.
_{Noun}

Mining Adventure (Part I)

Adjective _____

Noun _____

Verb ending in "-ing" _____

Adjective _____

Noun _____

Plural noun _____

Place _____

Noun _____

Number _____

Adjective _____

Verb ending in "-ing" _____

Animal sound (plural) _____

Noun _____

Noun _____

Plural noun _____

Mining Adventure (Part I)

It's a/an _____ morning, and the square
              Adjective

sun is just rising above the trees. Steve and his best

_____ Bleater decide it's a perfect day for
    Noun

_____. First, they gather the supplies they'll
Verb ending in "-ing"

need: several _____ pickaxes, food to give them
             Adjective

_____, and two stacks of _____,
   Noun   *Plural noun*

for light. Nearby, there is a/an _____ where
                            Place

they've already had good lucking finding coal and

_____ ore, enough to make _____
   Noun   *Number*

iron ingot(s). Steve leads the way inside and down the

_____ slope. "Come on, Bleater," he says,
   Adjective

"let's get _____!" The sheep _____
      Verb ending in "-ing"   *Animal sound (plural)*

his agreement, and passes a/an _____ to
                         Noun

Steve. Steve swings at the nearest _____,
                         Noun

and heavy _____ of cobblestone begin falling
      Plural noun

left and right.

Mining Adventure (Part II)

Exclamation! _____

Adjective _____

Plural noun _____

Noun _____

Adverb _____

Adjective _____

Adjective _____

Number _____

Adverb _____

Verb ending in "-ing" _____

Adjective _____

Adjective _____

Noun _____

Noun _____

Number _____

Mining Adventure (Part II)

"_____!" says Bleater. Steve looks, but
_{Exclamation!}

it is too _____ to see. He places a few
_{Adjective}

bright _____ around the _____.
_{Plural noun}   _{Noun}

"That's better. I just needed some more light,"

says Steve _____. In the clearing dust,
_{Adverb}

and the _____ torchlight, Steve sees
_{Adjective}

a/an _____ patch of iron. There are at least
_{Adjective}

_____ exposed ore block(s). "Iron!" he shouts
_{Number}

_____. Steve and Bleater smile at each other,
_{Adverb}

and then go to work _____ the ore. As they
_{Verb ending in "-ing"}

mine, they think of all the _____ stuff they
_{Adjective}

can craft with the iron. Steve dreams about

_____ armor or a shiny, iron _____.
_{Adjective}   _{Noun}

Bleater doesn't care what they make, as long as it isn't

_____. There is even more iron than they
_{Noun}

thought, and in the end, they mine enough to make

_____ ingot(s)!
_{Number}

Our House

Color _____

Adjective _____

Adjective _____

Adjective ending in "-er" _____

Number _____

Noun _____

Adjective _____

Noun _____

Type of container _____

Plural noun _____

Adjective _____

Mood _____

Noun _____

Our House

Bleater and I built a/an _____ house on a hill
Color

overlooking a/an _____ pool. We used to live
Adjective

in a/an _____ cave near the same pool, but
Adjective

decided we would upgrade to something

_____. The house has _____
Adjective ending in "-er" Number

room(s), and it is much nicer than the cave

we used to live in. Our house has a wooden

_____ to keep _____ mobs
Noun Adjective

out. Inside, we have a crafting _____, a
Noun

furnace, and a/an _____ to store our
Type of container

precious _____. I've been talking about build-
Plural noun

ing a/an _____ bed, but Bleater doesn't want
Adjective

to give me any of his wool. So instead, we just curl up

together in the noun. We're so _____ to have
Mood

a/an _____ of our own!
Noun

Cooking

Plural noun _____

Adjective _____

Plural noun _____

Plural noun _____

Plural noun _____

Plural noun _____

Exclamation! _____

Noun _____

Number _____

Plural noun _____

Noun _____

Noun _____

Part of Body _____

Cooking

What would life be without food? There is an abundance of tasty _____ to eat in the world. There
                Plural noun

are _____ crops you can farm, like carrots,
     Adjective

_____, pumpkins, and _____. And
Plural noun   Plural noun

there are animals you can eat, like pigs, _____,
                                 Plural noun

and _____. Yes, you can also eat sheep, but
    Plural noun

Bleater says "_____!" when I talk about that.
        Exclamation!

My favorite _____ of all time is definitely
         Noun

cake! I can eat _____ cake(s) every day. Cake
       Number

requires a lot of _____, including milk, eggs,
       Plural noun

_____, and _____.It's not very hard
Noun   Noun

to find the ingredients, and once you put it in your

_____, you'll never want anything else!
Part of body

Friendly Mobs (Part I)

Adjective _____

Animal (plural) _____

Animal (plural) _____

Adjective _____

Plural noun _____

Noun _____

Plural noun _____

Noun _____

Noun _____

Adjective _____

Noun _____

Animal _____

Verb ending in "-ing" _____

Adjective _____

Friendly Mobs (Part I)

There are lots of mobs in the world. Some are nice, and some are _____. It's good for you to know
Adjective

which will help you, and which will hurt you. Most animals are nice: cows, sheep, _____, pigs,
Animal (plural)

_____, and horses, for example, won't hurt
Animal (plural)

you. Some can even be _____. Chickens, for
Adjective

instance, lay _____, and can be mined for their
Plural noun

_____ and their feathers—great for making
Noun

_____. Cows are good eating, and they also
Plural noun

drop _____, so you can make some leather
Noun

_____. Horses are extra _____, be-
Noun   _Adjective_

cause you can ride them. But first you'll have to be lucky

enough to find a/an _____. Once you have a
Noun

saddle, you can tame a/an _____ and ride it
Animal

around! It's much faster than _____, and you
Verb ending in "-ing"

can jump super _____, too.
Adjective

Friendly Mobs (Part II)

Plural noun _____

Animal (plural) _____

Adjective _____

Adjective _____

Plural noun _____

Plural noun _____

Plural noun _____

Noun _____

Adjective _____

Plural Noun _____

Number _____

Verb ending in "-ing" _____

Plural noun _____

Adjective _____

Friendly Mobs (Part II)

There are a bunch of other _____ you can
_{Plural noun}
tame, if you know how. Donkeys and _____
_{Animal (plural)}
look different from horses, but they are _____.
_{Adjective}
Only horses can wear _____ armor. But
_{Adjective}
you can saddle all three, and donkeys and mules can

carry _____ full of _____ for you!
_{Plural noun} _{Plural noun}
Speaking of pack _____, llamas can also
_{Plural noun}
carry your _____ for you, and you can string
_{Noun}
them together in a/an _____ caravan, too.
_{Adjective}
If _____ aren't your thing, llamas also drop
_{Plural Noun}
leather. There are _____ more mob(s) you
_{Number}
can tame that are useful. Parrots alert you to danger by

_____ the sounds of hostile _____
_{Verb ending in "-ing"} _{Plural noun}
nearby. Wolves are a Steve's _____ friend
_{Adjective}
(except sheep!). Once tamed, wolves will fight to

protect you!

Sheep (Part I)

Adjective _____

Noun _____

Adjective _____

Adjective _____

Mood _____

Number _____

Adjective _____

Noun _____

Noun _____

Adjective _____

Noun _____

Adjective _____

Adverb _____

Plural noun _____

Sheep (Part I)

Let me tell you about sheep. They are one _____ animal. Bleater is a sheep, and he's
Adjective

my best _____. Sheep make great friends
Noun

because they are so _____. Bleater has
Adjective

stuck with me through _____ and thin. I'm
Adjective

never _____ when he's with me. Sheep are
Mood

your basic _____ legged beast with a/an
Number

_____ tail. It's hard to see the tail, but trust
Adjective

me, it's there. It's like a little puffy _____.
Noun

When their _____ grows out long their whole
Noun

bodies are super _____, and they look like
Adjective

giant balls of _____. Bleater makes a/an
Noun

_____ pillow when he's like this. And when
Adjective

sheep are _____ sheared, it turns out they're
Adverb

quite skinny (and hilarious-looking) _____.
Plural noun

Sheep (Part II)

Animals (plural) _____

Adjective _____

Plural noun _____

Plural noun _____

Exclamation! _____

Noun _____

Number _____

Adjective _____

Noun _____

Adjective _____

Mood _____

Animal _____

Adjective _____

Verb _____

Adjective _____

Sheep (Part II)

Who would have thought there was so much to know about _____? Some people think sheep are
Animals (plural)

not very _____, but that's not true! Sheep are
Adjective

brilliant thinkers and excellent _____! Bleater
Plural noun

is always coming up with amazing _____, and
Plural noun

whenever I'm about to do something stupid, he always

yells "_____!" to warn me. If you don't have
Exclamation!

a best _____ who is a sheep, I suggest you
Noun

get _____. They are the _____!
Number _Adjective_

There is one other _____ you need to
Noun

know. When sheep get wet, they get _____
Adjective

cranky. VERY, very _____. The smell of wet
Mood

_____ is very _____. My advice: try
Animal _Adjective_

to _____ your _____ friends dry at
Verb _Adjective_

all times!

Chickens

Adjective _____

Noun _____

Plural noun _____

Verb ending in "-ing" _____

Adjective _____

Plural noun _____

Noun _____

Unit of time _____

Adjective _____

Noun _____

Verb _____

Noun _____

Verb ending in "-ing" _____

Adjective _____

Hot place _____

Plural noun _____

Chickens

Chickens are perhaps the most _____ mob in
Adjective

the entire _____ of Minecraft. Chicken produce
Noun

_____ which are useful for cooking, but also
Plural noun

for _____ more chickens! It's _____
Verb ending in "-ing"   _Adjective_

to start a chicken farm with just a few _____,
Plural noun

and seeds you find in the _____. Feed your
Noun

chickens every _____, and you'll have a/an
Unit of time

_____ chicken _____ in no time.
Adjective   _Noun_

When you decide to _____ some of the chick-
Verb

ens, you'll always get _____ and feathers.
Noun

Not to mention that _____ chickens gives a
Verb ending in "-ing"

_____ amount of experience, too! You can
Adjective

cook the meat in a/an _____ to make food, and
Hot place

the feathers are always useful to craft _____.
Plural noun

Build your Chicken farm today!

Combat 101

Time of day _____

Adjective _____

Adjective _____

Noun _____

Noun _____

Body part _____

Verb with -ing _____

Adverb _____

Exclamation! _____

Exclamation! _____

Noun _____

Adjective _____

Noun _____

Exclamation! _____

Combat 101

Are you scared to go out at _____ because
Time of day
you don't know how to fight? No problem! Let me

give you a/an _____ fighting lesson. While
Adjective
it's true that you can fight with your _____
Adjective
fists, or a shovel, pickaxe, or _____, those are
Noun
really made to be tools. You need a sword. I don't

care if it's made of wood, stone, _____, or
Noun
diamond; just get something! Are you holding it in your

_____? Good. Now trying _____ it
Body part Verb with -ing
while _____ shouting "_____!" How
Adverb Exclamation!
did that feel? Try it again. _____! Now you're
Exclamation!
getting it! When you hit a/an _____ with your
Noun
sword, it will knock them back, giving you time to ready

another _____ swing. Now get out there and
Adjective
practice _____ fighting! _____!
Noun Exclamation!

Spiders

Adjective _____

Noun _____

Plural noun _____

Number _____

Color _____

Noun _____

Person in the room _____

Adjective _____

Adjective _____

Noun _____

Adverb _____

Noun _____

Noun _____

Body part _____

Adjective _____

Spiders

Spiders can't decide if they want to be friendly or

_____. At night, they will attack you just like
    Adjective

any other _____. They jump and hiss, they
              Noun

can climb _____, they have _____
        Plural noun   Number

leg(s) and so many gleaming _____ eyes.
                         Color

But then the _____ rises, and Spiders wan-
           Noun

der around pretending they weren't trying to eat

_____ all night. It's very _____!
Person in the room   Adjective

Because of the way they jump, it can be _____
                              Adjective

to fight a Spider with a/an _____. Spiders can
                    Noun

_____ slip through small spaces, and climb
   Adverb

the walls of your _____—so don't forget to
             Noun

build a/an _____. Spiders almost always drop
       Noun

their _____, but will sometimes drop string
     Body part

—a/an _____ crafting material to make bows.
     Adjective

Skeletons

Number _____

Body part _____

Person in the room _____

Adverb _____

Plural noun _____

Plural noun _____

Verb _____

Adjective _____

Adjective _____

Noun _____

Noun _____

Adjective _____

Noun _____

Exclamation! _____

Verb _____

Skeletons

Skeletons only have _____ thing(s) on their
_{Number}

_____, and that's finding _____
_{Body part} _{Person in the room}

and filling your hide full of arrows! They make look

slow, but they can move very _____.
_{Adverb}

Skeletons sometimes drop bows, and almost always

give you _____. They're also clever, and will
_{Plural noun}

hide behind _____ and trees, waiting for the
_{Plural noun}

best moment to _____. Your _____
_{Verb} _{Adjective}

strategy is to craft a/an _____ bow of your
_{Adjective}

own. If you don't have a bow, lead the Skeleton

around a tree or a/an _____. Then, when
_{Noun}

they come around the _____, slice them
_{Noun}

with your _____ sword. It helps to shout a
_{Adjective}

battle _____, like "_____!" What-
_{Noun} _{Exclamation!}

ever you do, don't give them time to _____
_{Verb}

you with arrows!

Zombies

Adjective _____

Person in the room_____

Noun _____

Noun _____

Noun _____

Place _____

Noun _____

Noun _____

Plural noun _____

Noun _____

Plural noun _____

Body part _____

Noun _____

Adjective _____

Plural noun _____

Zombies

Zombies are _____ and dumb, just like you
                    Adjective

might expect. But they can smell _____ from
                                  Person in the room

a mile away! More than any other _____,
                                   Noun

Zombies won't give up until they find you. They'll climb

on your _____. They'll even bang on your
         Noun

_____. You'll see them coming from across the
   Noun

_____, zig-zagging in your _____.
   Place   *Noun*

Fortunately this gives you plenty of _____
                                      Noun

to shoot them with _____. The only excep-
                    Plural noun

tion to this _____ is Baby Zombies. Those are
             Noun

some fast _____! They will run straight at you
          Plural noun

and start munching on your _____. While
                            Body part

Zombies mostly drop rotten _____, you can
                            Noun

sometimes get _____ and get armor—even
               Adjective

enchanted _____!
          Plural noun

Creepers

Adjective _____

Noun _____

Adjective _____

Exclamation! _____

Verb _____

Adjective _____

Verb ending in "-ing" _____

Verb _____

Adjective _____

Adjective _____

Body Part _____

Noun _____

Adjective _____

Creepers

Do you hear that _____ mob sneaking up
_{Adjective}
behind you? No! You don't! Because it's a Creep-
er, and just like their _____ suggests, the
_{Noun}
are _____ little critters. They walk with-
_{Adjective}
out making any noise until they're right next to you,
Then they say, "_____." And then they
_{Exclamation!}
_____. That's right, they explode. Creepers
_{Verb}
are especially _____ if you're not _____
_{Adjective} _{Verb ending in "-ing"}
armor. The worst thing about Creepers is that they can

_____ at any time, even during the day! The
_{Verb}
best way to protect yourself from Creepers is to wear

_____ armor, and remain _____.
_{Adjective} _{Adjective}
Keep a/an _____ on your surroundings, and if
_{Body Part}
you hear a/an _____, run like _____!
_{Noun} _{Adjective}

Endermen

Animal sound _____

Loud noise! _____

Body part _____

Noun _____

Body part _____

Mood _____

Adjective _____

Adjective _____

Verb _____

Adjective _____

Noun _____

Number _____

Place _____

Verb _____

Endermen

Nothing scares me quite like an Enderman. They

_____ while they're walking around, and
Animal sound

then _____, they teleport somewhere and
Loud noise!

VOOP, here they come back again. I try and keep my

_____ facing the _____ whenever
Body part   Noun

an Enderman is around. If you look an Enderman in the

_____ it makes them _____! Talk
Body part   Mood

about a/an _____ temper! And then they'll
Adjective

come after you with _____ fury. You can't
Adjective

run because VOOP. Don't even try to _____
Verb

them without _____ weapons and pow-
Adjective

erful _____. It seems like they have about
Noun

_____ heart(s)! If you want to escape an
Number

Enderman, leap into the nearest lake or _____.
Place

Endermen _____ water and won't follow you.
Verb

The Nether

Adjective _____

Adjective _____

Verb ending in "-ing" _____

Liquid _____

Adjective _____

Plural Noun _____

Adjective _____

Noun _____

Adjective _____

Plural noun _____

Adjective _____

Adjective _____

Adverb _____

Verb _____

Noun _____

The Nether

Don't ever go to the Nether! It's _____

Adjective

there! It's dark, hot, and _____. There are

Adjective

fires _____ everywhere. I hope you aren't

Verb ending in "-ing"

thirsty, because you won't find any _____

Liquid

there either. Do you hear that _____ noise?

Adjective

Don't be fooled. It's a Ghast! They fly around and shoot

_____. If you're _____ enough to find

Plural Noun · Adjective

a Nether Fortress, you're only in for more _____.

Noun

Wither Skeletons and Blazes spawn there. Sure, they

drop some _____ _____, but is it worth

Adjective · Plural noun

the trouble? By far, the most _____ mobs are

Adjective

the zombie pigmen. They look _____, but if

Adjective

you even _____ _____ one, they

Adverb · Verb

won't stop until you're dead! Take my _____,

Noun

and just stay out!

Made in the USA
San Bernardino,
CA